NANCY TUMINELLY

Cool

SUGAR-FREE RECIPES

DELICIOUS & FUN FOODS WITHOUT REFINED SUGAR

A Division of ABDO
ABDO
Publishing Company

visit us at www.abdopublishing.com

Published by ABDO Publishing Company, a division of ABDO, P.O. Box 398166, Minneapolis, Minnesota 55439. Copyright © 2013 by Abdo Consulting Group, Inc. International copyrights reserved in all countries. No part of this book may be reproduced in any form without written permission from the publisher. Checkerboard Library™ is a trademark and logo of ABDO Publishing Company.

Printed in the United States of America, North Mankato, Minnesota
102012
012013

 PRINTED ON RECYCLED PAPER

Design and Production: Mighty Media, Inc.
Series Editor: Liz Salzmann
Photo Credits: Aaron DeYoe, Shutterstock

The following manufacturers/names appearing in this book are trademarks: Panasonic®, Pyrex®, Kitchen Aid®, Arm & Hammer®, Kraft® Calumet®, Bob's Red Mill®, Roundy's®, Stevia in the Raw®, McCormick®, Stevita®, Minute Maid®, Jell-o®, Clara Ole®, Village Cannery®, Baker's®, Nestlé®, Pam®, Osterizer®

Library of Congress Cataloging-in-Publication Data

Tuminelly, Nancy, 1952-
  Cool sugar-free recipes : delicious & fun foods without refined sugar / Nancy Tuminelly.
     pages cm. -- (Cool recipes for your health)
  Audience: 8-12
  Includes bibliographical references and index.
  ISBN 978-1-61783-585-8
  1. Cooking--Juvenile literature. 2. Sugar-free diet--Recipes--Juvenile literature. I. Title.
   TX652.5.T8424 2013
   641.5'63837--dc23
                            2012024006

TO ADULT HELPERS

This is your chance to introduce newcomers to the fun of cooking! As children learn to cook, they develop new skills, gain confidence, and make some delicious food.

These recipes are designed to help children cook fun and healthy dishes. They may need more adult assistance for some recipes than others. Be there to offer help and guidance when needed, but encourage them to do as much as they can on their own. Also encourage them to be creative by using the variations listed or trying their own ideas. Building creativity into the cooking process encourages children to think like real chefs.

Before getting started, establish rules for using the kitchen, cooking tools, and ingredients. It is important for children to have adult supervision when using sharp tools, the oven, or the stove.

Most of all, be there to cheer on your new chefs. Put on your apron and stand by. Watch and learn. Taste their creations. Praise their efforts. Enjoy the culinary adventure!

CONTENTS

SUGAR-FREE

HIGH-FRUCTOSE CORN SYRUP is a type of sugar.
It is often in foods that aren't very sweet, such as bread or crackers.
Read the packaging and labels very carefully!

Everybody likes sugar! But eating too much sugar is bad for you. And for many people it is important to eat little or no sugar. Some people have a disease called ***diabetes***. Their bodies can't control how much sugar gets into their blood. They have to avoid eating sugar to keep their blood sugar level low.

Sugar is found naturally in many foods. Fruits, grains, and dairy products all contain natural sugar. Refined sugar is made from plants such as sugarcane and sugar beets. The natural sugar is taken from them and processed. It's made into the sugar people put in their coffee and use in baking. It is also added to commercially produced foods and drinks. When shopping, avoid foods made with refined sugar. Read the labels carefully.

Sometimes a recipe that includes refined sugar will list sugar-free **options** for those ingredients. Or, be creative and make up your own **variations**. Being a chef is all about using your imagination.

SAFETY FIRST!

Some recipes call for activities or ingredients that require caution. If you see these symbols, ask an adult for help!

Hot - This recipe requires handling hot objects. Always use oven mitts when holding hot pans.

Sharp - You need to use a sharp knife or cutting tool for this recipe. Ask an adult to help out.

Nuts - This recipe includes nuts. People who are allergic to nuts should not eat it.

THE BASICS

ASK PERMISSION

Before you cook, ask **permission** to use the kitchen, cooking tools, and ingredients. If you'd like to do something yourself, say so! If you would like help, ask for it!

BE NEAT AND CLEAN

- Start with clean hands, clean tools, and a clean work surface.
- Wear comfortable clothing.
- Tie back long hair and roll up your sleeves so they stay out of the food.

NO GERMS ALLOWED!

Raw eggs and raw meat have bacteria in them that can make you sick. After you handle raw eggs or meat, wash your hands, tools, and work surfaces with soap and water. Keep everything clean!

READ THESE IMPORTANT TIPS BEFORE YOU START!

BE PREPARED

- Be organized. Knowing where everything is makes cooking easier!
- Read the directions all the way through before you start cooking.
- Set out all your ingredients before starting.

BE SMART, BE SAFE

- Never work alone in the kitchen.
- Ask an adult before using anything hot or sharp, such as a stove top, oven, knife, or **grater**.
- Turn pot handles toward the back of the stove to avoid accidentally knocking them over.

MEASURING

Many ingredients are measured by the cup, tablespoon, or teaspoon. Some ingredients are measured by weight in ounces or pounds. You can buy food by its weight too.

THE TOOL BOX

3-INCH ROUND COOKIE CUTTER

9×5-INCH LOAF PAN

9×9-INCH BAKING DISH

ALUMINUM FOIL

BAKING SHEET

BLENDER

CUTTING BOARD

FONDUE POT

FORK

MEASURING CUPS

MEASURING SPOONS

MICROWAVE-SAFE BOWL

The tools you will need for the recipes in this book are listed below. When a recipe says to use a tool you don't recognize, turn back to these pages to see what it looks like.

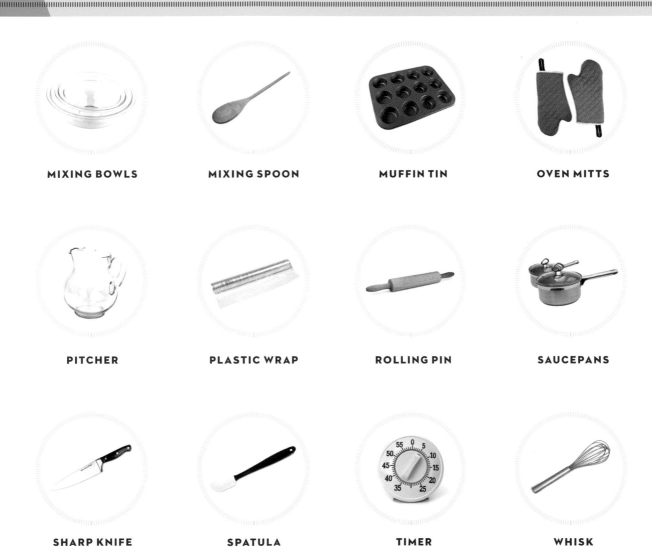

MIXING BOWLS

MIXING SPOON

MUFFIN TIN

OVEN MITTS

PITCHER

PLASTIC WRAP

ROLLING PIN

SAUCEPANS

SHARP KNIFE

SPATULA

TIMER

WHISK

COOL INGREDIENTS

BAKING SODA & POWDER

BANANAS

BROWN RICE FLOUR

CREAM CHEESE

DRIED APRICOTS

EGGS

GRANULATED ARTIFICIAL SWEETENER

GROUND CINNAMON

GROUND NUTMEG

LEMON EXTRACT

LIQUID SWEETENER

LITE WHIPPED TOPPING

Many of these recipes call for basic ingredients such as milk, vegetable oil, non-stick cooking spray, all-purpose flour, ice, salt, and butter. Here are other ingredients needed for the recipes in this book.

NUTS
(PECANS & WALNUTS)

ORANGE JUICE
CONCENTRATE

PUMPKIN PIE SPICE

RAISINS

STRAWBERRIES

SUGAR-FREE INSTANT
VANILLA PUDDING MIX

SUGAR-FREE
MAPLE SYRUP

UNSWEETENED
APPLESAUCE

UNSWEETENED
CHOCOLATE SQUARES

UNSWEETENED
COCOA POWDER

VANILLA EXTRACT

WHITE RICE

COOKING TERMS

ARRANGE

Arrange means to place things in a certain order or pattern.

BOIL

Boil means to heat liquid until it begins to bubble.

CHOP

Chop means to cut into small pieces.

FLUFF

Fluff means to loosen or separate using a fork.

GREASE

Grease means to coat something with butter, oil, or cooking spray.

Always wash fruit and vegetables well. Rinse them under cold water.
Pat them dry with a **towel**. Then they won't slip when you cut them.

MASH

Mash means to press down and smash food with a fork.

SLICE

Slice means to cut food into pieces of the same thickness.

SPREAD

Spread means to make a smooth layer with a spoon, knife, or spatula.

STIR

Stir means to mix ingredients together, usually with a large spoon.

WHISK

Whisk means to beat quickly by hand with a whisk or fork.

RICE PUDDING

makes 6 servings

INGREDIENTS

non-stick cooking spray

2 cups white rice

salt

1⅓ cups milk ✳

½ cup sugar-free maple syrup

1 tablespoon butter, softened ✳

1 tablespoon granulated artificial sweetener

1 teaspoon vanilla extract

1 teaspoon ground cinnamon

3 eggs

⅓ cup raisins (optional) ✳

TOOLS

9×9-inch baking dish

measuring cups & spoons

medium saucepan

fork

large mixing bowl

mixing spoon

spatula

oven mitts

timer

✳ contains natural sugar

14

1. Preheat the oven to 325 degrees. Coat the baking dish with cooking spray. Set it aside.

2. Put the rice, 1 teaspoon salt, and 3 cups water in a medium saucepan. Bring to a boil over medium-high heat.

3. Cover the saucepan and turn the heat to low. Let the rice cook for 18 minutes. Do not remove the lid.

4. Turn off the heat and let the rice sit for 10 minutes.

5. Take the lid off the pan. Use a fork to fluff the rice. Put the rice in a large mixing bowl.

6. Add the remaining ingredients plus $\frac{1}{8}$ teaspoon salt to the rice. Stir with a mixing spoon for 5 to 10 minutes.

7. Put the rice mixture in the baking dish. Spread it evenly with the spatula. Bake for 50 minutes. Let it cool for 30 minutes before serving.

CELEBRATION CAKE

makes 12 servings

INGREDIENTS

CAKE

non-stick cooking spray
2 cups raisins *
1 cup chopped walnuts
2 cups all-purpose flour
1 teaspoon baking soda
½ teaspoon salt
1½ teaspoons ground cinnamon
½ teaspoon ground nutmeg
2 eggs
1 cup unsweetened applesauce *
¾ cup vegetable oil
1 teaspoon vanilla extract
3 tablespoons liquid sweetener

FROSTING

1.4 ounces sugar-free instant vanilla pudding mix
1¾ cups milk *
8 ounces cream cheese, softened *
8 ounces lite whipped topping *

TOOLS

9×9-inch baking dish
measuring cups & spoons
medium saucepan
mixing bowls
mixing spoon
oven mitts
spatula
timer   * contains natural sugar

THIS CAKE WILL GIVE YOU A REASON TO PARTY!

1. Preheat the oven to 350 degrees. Coat the baking dish with cooking spray.

2. Put the raisins and 3 cups water in a medium saucepan. Heat over medium-low heat, stirring constantly. Remove the pan from the heat when the water is gone.

3. Put the raisins in a medium bowl and let them cool. Then mix in the walnuts, flour, baking soda, salt, cinnamon, and nutmeg. In a large bowl, mix together the eggs, applesauce, vegetable oil, vanilla, and liquid sweetener.

4. Pour the raisin mixture into the egg mixture. Stir well. Pour it into the baking dish. Bake for 60 minutes. Let the cake cool.

5. Put the pudding mix and milk in a medium bowl. Stir until thick. In a large bowl, stir the cream cheese until it's smooth. Add the pudding mixture. Stir well. Mix in the whipped topping.

6. Spread the frosting on the cake with a spatula.

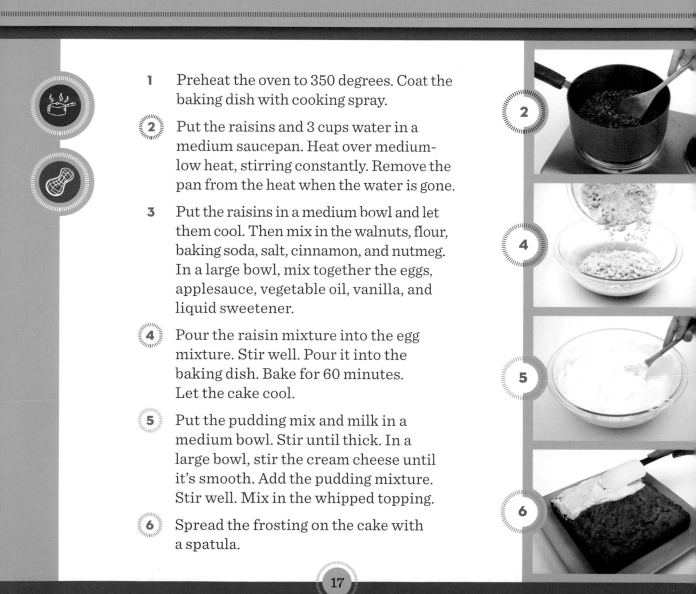

MARVELOUS MUFFINS

makes 12 muffins

INGREDIENTS

non-stick cooking spray

1 egg

1 cup milk *

1 tablespoon vegetable oil

2 cups brown rice flour

2 teaspoons baking powder

4 tablespoons granulated artificial sweetener

TOOLS

muffin tin

mixing bowls

whisk

measuring cups & spoons

mixing spoon

oven mitts

timer

* contains natural sugar

1. Preheat the oven to 350 degrees. Coat the muffin tin with cooking spray. Set it aside.

2. Crack the egg into a large mixing bowl. Make sure not to get any shell in the bowl! Whisk the egg for about a minute. Stir in the milk and oil.

3. In a medium bowl, mix together the flour, baking powder, and artificial sweetener.

4. Slowly add the flour mixture to the egg mixture. Stir well.

5. Fill each cup of the muffin tin, about ¾ full. Bake for 25 minutes.

6. Remove the muffins from the oven. Let them cool before eating. Serve with butter.

PARADISE SMOOTHIE

makes 2 servings

INGREDIENTS

2 bananas *

2 cups strawberries *

½ cup milk *

1 teaspoon of
vanilla extract

2 cups ice, crushed

TOOLS

measuring cups & spoons

sharp knife

cutting board

blender

bowl

2 glasses

* contains natural sugar

1. Chop off the tops of the strawberries. Slice the strawberries in half.

2. Put the chopped strawberries in a bowl. Freeze for 1 hour.

3. Take the bowl out of the freezer. Chop the bananas and add to bowl.

4. Dump the bowl of fruit into a blender. Add the milk, vanilla, and ice.

5. Blend for 5 minutes or until smooth.

6. Pour into the glasses. Drink up this summer classic!

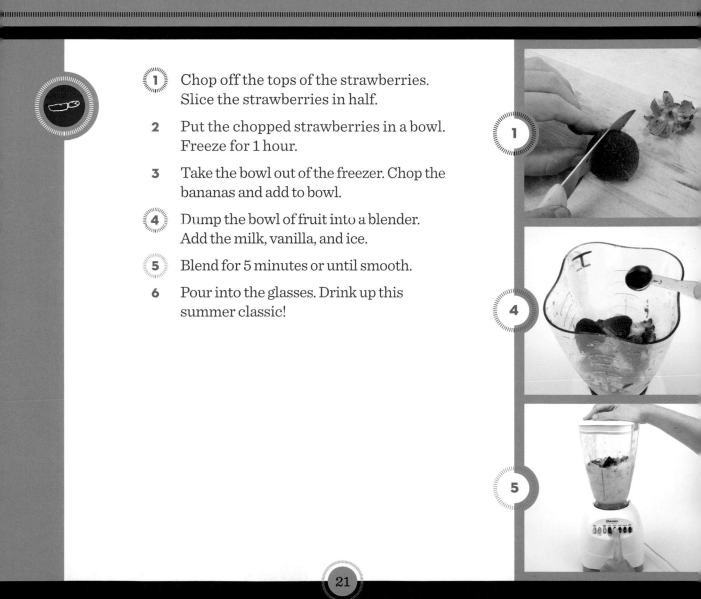

CHOCOLATE FUDGE

makes 16 servings

INGREDIENTS

2 ounces unsweetened chocolate squares

16 ounces cream cheese, softened *

½ cup granulated artificial sweetener

1 teaspoon vanilla extract

½ cup pecans, chopped

TOOLS

9×9-inch baking dish

aluminum foil

small microwave-safe bowl

measuring cups & spoons

medium mixing bowl

mixing spoon

sharp knife

plastic wrap

* contains natural sugar

1. Line the baking pan with aluminum foil. Set it aside.

2. Put the unsweetened chocolate in a small bowl. Melt the chocolate in the microwave. Wait for it to cool.

3. Put the chocolate, cream cheese, artificial sweetener, and vanilla in a medium bowl. Stir well. Mix in the pecans.

4. Pour the chocolate mixture into the dish. Spread it evenly. Cover the dish with plastic wrap. Put it in the refrigerator overnight.

5. Cut the fudge into squares. Store it in the refrigerator.

--- EVEN COOLER! ---

Add cranberries, apricots, or raisins for extra flavor!

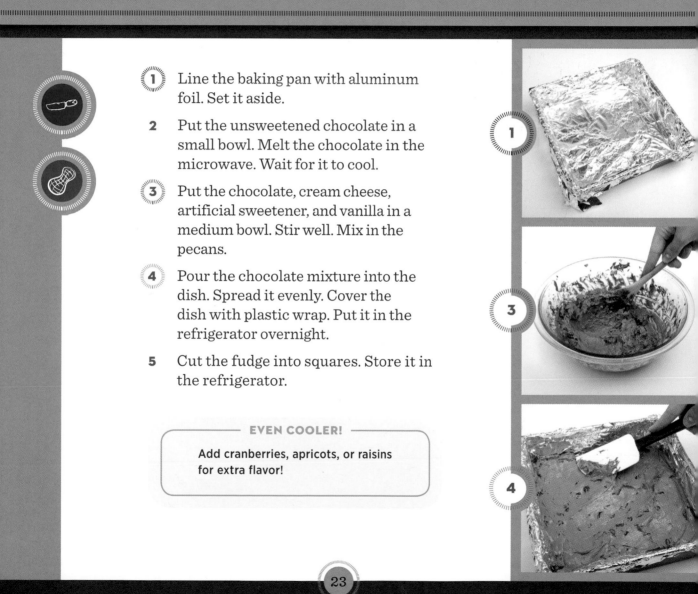

FLAVORFUL BREAD

makes 12 servings

INGREDIENTS

non-stick cooking spray

2 cups all-purpose flour

1½ teaspoons pumpkin pie spice

1 teaspoon baking soda

½ teaspoon salt

1 teaspoon baking powder

1 cup bananas, mashed *

6-ounce can orange juice concentrate, thawed *

2 eggs

1 cup raisins *

½ teaspoon lemon extract

TOOLS

9×5-inch loaf pan

measuring cups & spoons

large mixing bowl

mixing spoon

oven mitts

sharp knife

cutting board

* contains natural sugar

1. Preheat the oven to 350 degrees. Coat the loaf pan with cooking spray. Set it aside.

2. Put the flour, pumpkin pie spice, baking soda, salt, and baking powder in a large bowl. Stir with mixing spoon.

3. Add the bananas, orange juice, eggs, raisins, and lemon extract. Stir well.

4. Pour the batter into the loaf pan. Make sure it is spread evenly.

5. Bake for 40 minutes, or until the loaf turns brown.

6. Remove the loaf from the oven. Let it cool for 10 minutes. Take the loaf out of the pan. Cut it into slices to share!

CHOCOLATE FONDUE

makes 8 servings

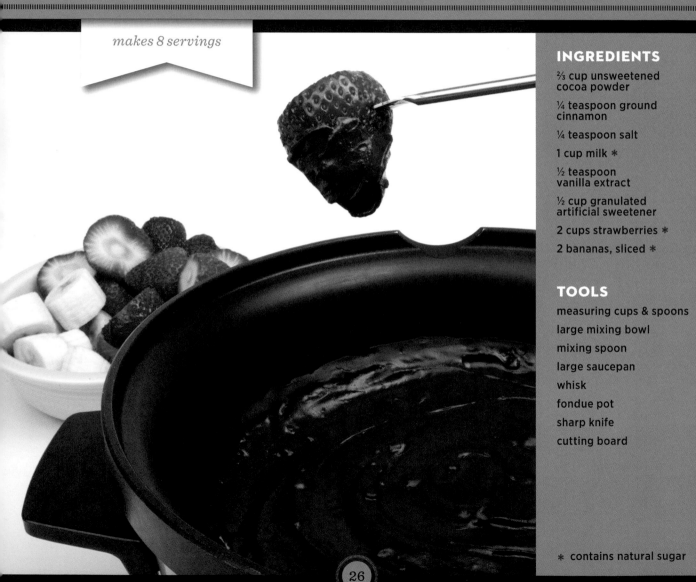

INGREDIENTS

⅔ cup unsweetened cocoa powder

¼ teaspoon ground cinnamon

¼ teaspoon salt

1 cup milk *

½ teaspoon vanilla extract

½ cup granulated artificial sweetener

2 cups strawberries *

2 bananas, sliced *

TOOLS

measuring cups & spoons

large mixing bowl

mixing spoon

large saucepan

whisk

fondue pot

sharp knife

cutting board

* contains natural sugar

1 Put the cocoa powder, cinnamon, salt, and milk in a large bowl. Stir well.

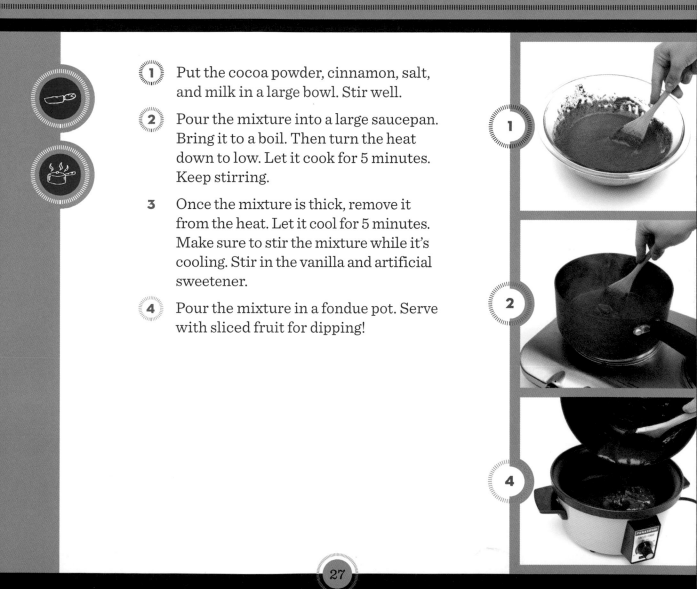

2 Pour the mixture into a large saucepan. Bring it to a boil. Then turn the heat down to low. Let it cook for 5 minutes. Keep stirring.

3 Once the mixture is thick, remove it from the heat. Let it cool for 5 minutes. Make sure to stir the mixture while it's cooling. Stir in the vanilla and artificial sweetener.

4 Pour the mixture in a fondue pot. Serve with sliced fruit for dipping!

COOKIE SURPRISE

makes 24 servings

INGREDIENTS

1 cup butter, softened *

1 three-ounce package cream cheese, softened *

¼ teaspoon vanilla extract

¼ teaspoon salt

2 cups all-purpose flour

1 cup of granulated artificial sweetener

24 dried apricots *

TOOLS

measuring cups & spoons

large mixing bowl

mixing spoon

rolling pin

3-inch round cookie cutter

baking sheet

oven mitts

timer

* contains natural sugar

1 Preheat the oven to 350 degrees.

2 Put the butter and cream cheese in a large bowl. Stir until **fluffy**.

3 Add the vanilla, salt, flour, and artificial sweetener. Stir well.

4 Make sure the counter is clean and dry. Then sprinkle it with flour. Put the cookie dough on the floured area. Roll out the dough with a rolling pin.

5 Use the cookie cutter to cut out circles of dough. Cut as many as you can out of the dough. You will need to roll the dough again several times.

6 Put a dried apricot on one of the circles. Put another circle on the top. Press the edges of the dough together around the apricot. Repeat until you've used all of the circles.

7 Arrange the cookies on a baking sheet. Bake for 10 minutes. Take the cookies out of the oven. Let them cool.

3

4

6

more about
SUGAR-FREE LIFE

If you liked these dishes, look for other sugar-free foods. If you want or need to avoid eating sugar, you have a lot of **options**!

Many people like to snack on sweet foods. Keep your kitchen stocked with nuts or vegetables as refined sugar-free **alternatives** for sugary snacks. Some refined sugar substitutes to have around the house include sugar-free maple syrup and artificial sweeteners.

Now you're ready to start making your own sugar-free recipes. It takes creativity and planning. Check out different cookbooks. Look through the lists of ingredients. You'll be surprised how many dishes don't need sugar. Or you can come up with your own recipes or **variations**. The kitchen is calling!

Most sugar substitutes are neither bad nor good for you. But it's best to eat sweet snacks in moderation no matter how they are sweetened.

GLOSSARY

ALTERNATIVE - something you can choose instead.

DIABETES - a disease that causes the level of sugar in the blood to be too high.

FLUFFY - light, soft, and airy.

GRATER - a tool with rough-edged holes used to shred something into small pieces.

OPTION - something you can choose.

PERMISSION - when a person in charge says it's okay to do something.

TOWEL - a cloth or paper used for cleaning or drying.

VARIATION - a change in form, position, or condition.

WEB SITES

To learn more about cooking for your health, visit ABDO Publishing Company on the Internet at www.abdopublishing.com. Web sites about creative ways for kids to cook healthy food are featured on our Book Links page. These links are routinely monitored and updated to provide the most current information available.

INDEX